A Colored Man's Journey Through 20th Century Segregated America

Earl Hutchinson, Sr.
with Earl Ofari Hutchinson

Middle Passage Press, Inc.
Los Angeles, CA

B HUTCHINSON

Books may be purchased for educationals, business, or sales promotional
use. For information please write: Middle Passage Press, Inc., 5517 Secrest
Drive, Los Angeles, CA 90043.

Publisher's Cataloging-in-Publication
(Provided by Quality Books, Inc.)

Hutchinson, Earl, 1903-
    A colored man's journey through 20th century
    segregated America / by Earl Hutchinson, Sr. —
    1st ed.
    p. cm.
    LCCN : 99-80024
    ISBN : 1-881032-17-5

    1. Hutchinson, Earl, 1903- 2. Afro-American—
Biography. 3. United States—History—20th
century.   I. Title.

E185.97.H88A3 2000   305.896/073/0092
                              QBI99-500569

A Word of Thanks

Several people have generously contributed their time, energy, love, and devotion to help me tell of my journey through 20th Century segregated America.

Above all, the first person I must thank is my dear and loving wife Dorothy (Kathy) Hutchinson. Next, I thank my son, Earl Ofari Hutchinson and my daughter-in-law, Barbara Bramwell-Hutchinson. Finally, I thank Juanita Shellie Daniels and Barbara Glass as well as the countless friends, relatives, and associates who have had a profound impact on my life.

May God continue to bless you all.

Dedication

A Tribute to My Family

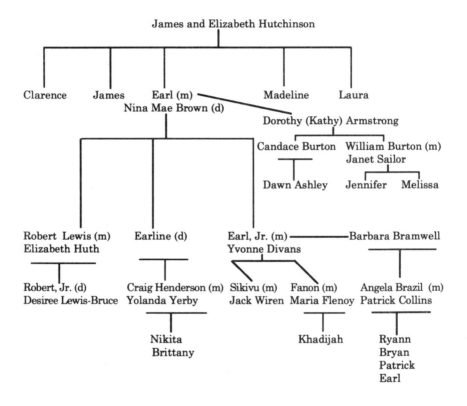

My family made me what I am. For that, I will be eternally thankful to the all merciful and benevolent God for blessing me with them.

Contents

My Eyewitness Journey Through 20th Century Segregated America

---

1903
- The publication of *The Souls of Black Folks* by W.E.B. DuBois was published.

1904
- Theodore Roosevelt was elected president.

1905
- The Niagara Movement, a political action organization founded by W.E. B. DuBois and William Monroe Trotter. It was the forerunner of the NAACP.

1908
- William Howard Taft was elected president.

- John Arthur Johnson, know as Jack Johnson, knocked out Tommy Burns in Sidney, Australia and became the first Negro to win the heavyweight boxing championship.

Earl Hutchinson, Sr.

1909
- The NAACP was founded.

1912
- Woodrow Wilson was elected president.

1915
- The Ku Klux Klan was reorganized and became a powerful force in American life.

- The number of Negroes migrating to the North increased.

1916
- Woodrow Wilson was re-elected president.

1917
- The United States entered World War I.

- The NAACP staged the Negro Silent Protest Parade and led thousands of Negroes in a march in New York to protest lynchings to critize the unwillingness of the federal government to end lynchings.

- The Supreme Court declared that cities could not legally require Negroes and whites to live on separate blocks.

- Marcus Garvey founded the Universal Negro Improvement Association in New York. Thousands of Negroes embraced his race pride message.

1918
- Negroes received decorations from the French and U.S. governments for bravery in combat.

My Eyewitness Journey

1919
- Negroes fought back in race riots in Washington, D.C., Chicago, IL, and other cities.

1920
- Warren G. Harding was elected president.

1924
- Calvin Cooledge was elected president.

1928
- Herbert Hoover was elected president.

1929
- Oscar Stanton DePriest became the first colored person elected to Congress since 1901.

- The Stock market collapsed.

1930
- The Great Depression began.

1931
- The Scottsboro boys were tried for raping two white women. Their scheduled execution touched off world-wide protests.

1932
- Franklin Delano Roosevelt was elected president.

1933
- Singer-actor-political activist Paul Robeson starred in the film *Emperor Jones*. He first appeared in the stage production in 1924.

Earl Hutchinson, Sr.

1934
- Arthur L. Mitchell defeated Oscar DePriest for Congress. He became the first Negro elected to Congress as a Democrat.

1936
- James Cleveland Owens, known as Jesse Owens, won four gold medals at the 1936 Olympics. His performance exploded the myth of black inferiority and angered Adolf Hitler.

- FDR was re-elected president.

1937
- Joe Louis knocked out James J. Braddock to become the heavyweight champion.

1939
- Marion Anderson sang before thousands at the Washington Monument in Washington, D.C.

1940
- FDR was re-elected president.

1941
- The Japanese attacked Pearl Harbor and the U.S. entered World War II.

- The first blacks were admitted to a segregated unit of the Army Air Corps.

- A. Philip Randolph called for a massive March on Washington, D.C. to protest employment discrimination.

- FDR signed Executive Order 8802 banning discrimination in the war industries. Randolph called off the March.

My <u>Eyewitness</u> Journey

1942
• William L. Dawson was elected to Congress from Chicago, IL.

1943
• This year marked one of the worst race riots of the war was in Detroit where thousands of Negroes and whites were killed or injured over the controversary of employment of blacks.

1944
• FDR was re-elected president.

1945
• More than one million colored men and women served in the armed forces. For the first time many of them saw combat in integrated units in battles in Europe and the Pacific. They performed with great distinction. It would take many years before the government finally recognized their achievements and awarded them the nation's highest honors.

• FDR died.

1946
• Vice President Harry Truman assumed the office of presidency.

1947
• Jackie Robinson became the first colored man in major league baseball this century.

1948
• Truman was elected president.

• Truman signed an executive order that integrated the armed forces.

- The Supreme Court in *Shelley v. Kraemer* declared that racially restrictive covenants in housing deeds were unforceable.

1951
- Mobs prevented a black family from moving into a white neighborhood in Cicero, IL.

1952
- Dwight D. Eisenhower was elected president.

1954
- The Supreme Court outlawed school segregation in *Brown v. Board of Education.*

1955
- Emmett Louis Till was lynched in Mississippi. Thousands turned out for his funeral in Chicago, IL. The U.S. Congress included a provision for federal investigations of civil rights violations in the Civil Rights Act of 1957.

- Nearly all the Negro baseball leagues teams had gone under.

1956
- Dwight D. Eisenhower was re-elected president.

1957
- Martin Luther King led the boycott against segregated buses in Montgomery, Alabama.

- Eisenhower ordered the use of federal troops to quell mobs trying to prevent Negro students from integrating Central High School in Little Rock, Arkansas.

My Eyewitness Journey

1960
- Student sit-ins began against segregated restaurants and public facilities in the South.

1961
- Interstate Commerce Commission outlawed segregation on buses and in terminals.

- John F. Kennedy was elected president.

1962
- Kennedy introduced his civil rights bill in Congress.

1963
- In a national radio address, Kennedy became the first U.S. president to tell Americans that segregation was "morally wrong."

- More than 250,000 persons participated in the March on Washington, D.C.

- Kennedy was assassinated in Dallas, TX.

1964
- Lyndon B. Johnson was elected president.

- The Civil Rights Bill was signed. This ended legal segregation in America.

Earl Hutchinson, Sr.

Introduction

A Note on Being "Colored" in 20th Century Segregated America

I do not intend for this book to be an exhaustive, in-depth look at the black experience in America. There have been legions of scholarly works that have dissected every aspect of our experience. I do intend for this book to be my personal recollections and impressions of the people, places, and events that shaped and influenced my life and that of millions of other Negroes in 20th Century segregated America.

I have been deeply blessed by God almighty to see the dawn of the 20th and the 21st Century. I was born in 1903. I lived through the terrible years when in the immortal words uttered by U.S. Supreme Court Chief Justice Roger

Taney in the *Dred Scott v. Sanford* decision in 1857 that blacks had no rights a white man was bound to respect. I have lived through the years when America did everything it could in law and practice to live up to those words. I have lived to see the great movements of social change in America that guaranteed people of color their legal rights. I have lived to see many of those monumental improvements and have known many of the people that helped make them. I have lived to see colored people called "ex-slaves," "colored," "negro," "Negro," "black," "Afro-American," and "African-American."

This is why I chose to title my book *A Colored Man's Journey Through 20th Century Segregated America.* In the era I lived through we called ourselves, Colored. We were proud of being colored. We turned the word into a badge of pride rather than an emblem of shame. It still is to me.

It is my fervent hope and prayer that in the 21st Century we will be called and treated as what we have always been namely, American.

1

THE PROMISED LAND

Father we know in the midst of every dark and dangeous situation in which we find our selves is thy invisible, yet strong hand, wise to lead, powerful to save by which a miraculous deliverance may be obtained.

*I*began my journey through 20th Century segregated America at the dawn of the 20th Century in 1903. Two things happened in that year that would have a towering impact on the 20th Century and an equally great affect on my life. A week after I was born in December the Wright Brothers took off on their solo flights on the sandy dunes of Kill Devil Hill and Kitty Hawk, North Carolina. I can still remember my mother, Elizabeth Hutchinson and my father Jim, talking excitedly about their flight a few years afterwards. She was amazed and fascinated at the idea that men could fly through the air like birds.

The Wright brothers' aircraft was the first of the great inventions that changed the shape of the 20th Century. During my life I would witness all of them. They would amaze and fascinate me, too.

A second thing happened the year I was born that would deeply affect my life and millions of other colored people everywhere. Eight months before my birth, Dr. W.E.B. DuBois published his magnificent work, *The Souls of Black Folk*. It was a slender book, in which he reflected on race in America. The book contained these prophetic words: "The problem of the 20th Century is the problem of the color line." Even DuBois couldn't know the pain, suffering, turmoil, and tumult that prediction would cause in the 20th Century.

I didn't have to look any further than the town I was born in, Clarksville, Tennessee, to see the impact his prophecy would have on the lives of colored and whites in America. The town was located on the Cumberland and Red Rivers in the Northwest corner of Tennessee. Clarksville was a leading livestock and farm goods producing area for that part of the country. It was also a leader in the manufacture of snuff. I was told that nearly everyone in town used it. They would spend many hours dipping and jamming the stuff up their noses. They said that you could often hear the whole town sneezing at one time.

In the small colored section of town where I was born, the trade store was colored-owned and the clerk was colored. It sold everything from food to clothes. The insurance company my mother paid her life insurance policy to was colored-owned. The livery stable was colored-owned. The funeral home was colored-owned. The cemetery was all-colored. The two or three chicken shacks were colored-owned. Everyone in the church where we ate, played, and prayed from early morning until late evening was colored. My parents knew every colored person in town. They spoke and visited with each other. They shared food with each other. They sat on the tiny slanted wooden stoops that passed for front porches on brutally hot summer nights; drank lemonade and soda, swapped stories, while they furiously fanned themselves.

I would sometimes hear them talk about white folks. But since I rarely saw one, they seemed as far from my life as the Sun and the Moon. The only time that changed was when the neighbors would drop their voices and say what a shame it was what they did to him. They never said who the "they" and the "him" was. Some years later after we had moved from Clarksville to St. Louis, I figured out who the "they" and the "him" were and what the "shame" was. The "they" were white mobs. The "him" was a black man or woman that they had lynched.

Lynchings were an almost everyday occurrence in America then. By the time I was ten-years-old more than 1000 blacks had been lynched. Lynch mobs riddled their colored victims with bullets, burned them at the stake, and hacked them to pieces. Often a whole town of whites would turn out to see a lynching. They would turn their gruesome work into a spectacle. Some would pack picnic lunches, and politicians and some businesspersons would show up to make speeches. In some places they put advertisements in local newspapers announcing the lynching. A lynching that happened anywhere in the country made many colored people even more terrified of whites.

Once I saw a picture in the *St. Louis Argus*, the city's colored newspaper, that my father would bring home. The picture was of a mob of whites standing around leering, joking, smiling, and mugging for the camera. They pointed to a body of a black man burning to death on an open fire.

We knew that the local sheriffs and politicians in those places wouldn't do anything to stop the lynchings or arrest the lynchers. But some colored people hoped that the president might do something about it.

14

The Promised Land

The presidents in the first decade of my life were Theodore Roosevelt and William Howard Taft. Many colored were especially hopeful about Roosevelt. He seemed to like colored people or at least some thought he did when he invited Negro educator Booker T. Washington to eat with him at the White House. They were even more hopeful when he appointed a few blacks to postmasterships in a few Southern towns.

This was the least he could do for us since nearly every colored person then that could vote, voted Republican. As it turned out Roosevelt wasn't going to do any more than the little he did for us. He wouldn't risk offending the South. And since none of the colored in Clarksville could vote, the Southern whites did anything they wanted to us.

And why not? In those days newspapers and magazines routinely printed stories in which they ridiculed us as "darkey," "mammy," "buck," "coon," and of course, "nigger." They depicted us as apes, baboons, and monkeys. They sang songs with titles such as "All Coons Look Alike To Me." Three years before I was born, a white writer, Charles Carroll, even titled his book *The Negro a Beast or In the Image of God*. This pretty much captured the thinking of many whites in those days.

Earl Hutchinson, Sr.

*M*y life in Clarksville ended before my first birthday. I later learned that my mother, had packed my things in a small cloth case, and sat it next to a few ruffled bags at the door. Then my father said to my mother "let's go." That was the start of my first journey through segregated America. Thousands of other blacks would make that same journey during the first two decades of the 20th Century. They were headed to the North, the promised land, where they hoped to escape from the poverty and violence that was an everyday part of their lives in the South.

We boarded a train and quickly moved to the colored section of the cars. The seats in this section were little more than wooden benches. They were in a wretched state of disrepair—broken and splintered.

The rule then was that once the train got across the Mason-Dixon line into the North that colored could sit anywhere they wanted—if there was a seat available. But there was almost never a seat available for a colored person in another section of the train. And most of the colored knew it and didn't even bother to try and move. At each stop along the way, a procession of colored men, women, small children, in fact entire families, would get on the train.

They were leaving their homes, friends, relatives, and acquaintances for good. They had baskets stuffed with fried chicken. They carried all types and sizes of bags and toted every kind of household item, including lamps, pictures, and small chests. These were all their worldly belongings and they were determined to take them with them to their new homes. There were so many colored heading North that in some small towns the colored section almost emptied out. By the end of World War I anywhere from 300,000 to a million colored had left the South for the North.

Many of them, like us, were heading for St. Louis. When the train pulled into the station many quickly jumped up and lined the aisles to get off. This was the first real city that many of them had ever seen. The first thing you noticed about the city was the noise and the endless throngs of people, colored and white, rushing back and forth on the streets. There were probably more people than ever in the city then because the year we arrived, 1904, was the year St. Louis hosted the Olympic Games and the World's Fair.

Whenever I looked out on the Mississippi River I saw huge paddle boats ferrying people up and down the river, and across from St. Louis to the other side of the river. This was before they built the bridge. The colored rode the boats on Monday nights. That was "colored night." They could gamble and listen to the music of Fate Marable's great band and Charley Creath's colored orchestra.

The huge number of blacks that were pouring into cities like St. Louis swelled the colored section. It seemed there was always a chronic housing shortage. Many of the new arrivals were forced to live with relatives and friends in crowded apartment buildings. The landlords would often slice up the apartment flats into boarding rooms to squeeze in as many people as they could, for a steep price, of course.

We moved into a small house near Natural Bridge and Ashland Avenues which then was the heart of the colored section. It was here that I first noticed one of the crazy quirks of segregation. There were no formal laws designating where colored and whites could or couldn't live. Yet all the whites lived on one side of the street and the colored lived on the other. They'd look at us and we'd look at them across the street. They wouldn't live on our side of the street and we couldn't live on their side of the street. But their kids would play with us. For a time many of my friends were white.

By the start of World War I that changed. St. Louis and dozens of other cities in the South and the North, passed city ordinances that forbade colored from living on blocks that were officially designated as "white blocks."

Some colored people protested this. I heard my mother and her friends mention the word NAACP and the name W.E.B. DuBois. They would say with an excited note in their voice that the NAACP was a colored group that was fighting for the colored people. The only other time I remember them getting that excited was when they talked about Jack Johnson in 1908. That was the year he knocked out Tommy Burns in Australia to become the first black heavyweight champion of the world.

But their mention of DuBois and the NAACP made me curious. Everytime I heard them mention them I listened even closer to find out more about this group that would fight for the colored. Yet things looked the same to me. I still walked past the local swimming pool. I'd see white kids jumping around and screaming in the pools on those hot summer days. I wished that I could be in there with them. I still couldn't go to a library or eat at any of the stores downtown. My mother still couldn't try on a dress in those stores.

There was only one high school for colored. I had to walk about three miles to school and back. I had to fight or run each way as I would be attacked by four or more white boys hollering: "Get the Nigger." Sometimes I would arrive home with a bloody nose. There were times when we would go to a nearby park to play. When the white kids saw us, they would always try to chase us out of there.

Despite the NAACP I still lived in a totally black world. It didn't seem that would ever change.

Earl Hutchinson, Sr.

2

DEMOCRACY FOR WHOM?

*O Lord our God, from who comes every blessing of spirit,
mind, and body, fill now our hearts with a living, constant,
spirit of gratitude and thanksgiving, that we may rightly
acknowledge thy blessings, and praise thy name, and attune
our lives to thy eternal life in all its beauty, glory,
joy and goodness.*

I could usually tell when something important had happened by the excitement in the voices and the lively expressions on the face of my parents and our neighbors when they talked. The thing that they were excited about this time was America's entrance into World War I. I began seeing black men on the streets wearing identical suits and caps. They walked with a swagger and had a determined look on their faces. Many of them hung out at the bars that were on the corner of nearly every block in our neighborhood.

They would be in there smoking, drinking, shouting, and laughing until the early morning hours. Wherever they went, people would pat them on the back and hug them. They would invite them over to their places for chicken and ham dinners, and ply them with plenty of drink. They were our heroes. They were the men who would march off to fight the Germans. Everyone was proud of them not only because they wore a uniform but because they would show the world that colored men could and would fight to make the world safe for democracy.

All the colored leaders and the colored newspapers carried stories about the war and how it was the duty of colored men to fight for their country. I saw pictures in the *Argus* of colored men dressed in snappy looking uniforms standing near airplanes, marching, drilling, standing next to artillery guns, and shouldering rifles at training camps.

I recall one headline in particular that filled up the whole front page of the paper. It read: "DUBOIS SAYS CLOSE RANKS." That was taken from an article DuBois wrote in the NAACP's *Crisis* magazine in 1918. It was read and circulated in most colored homes. The *Argus*, and I'm sure every Negro paper in the country, reprinted DuBois's article. He wanted the colored to support the war since he believed it was our fight, too. We all agreed with him.

---

*A*lthough everyone on my block stuck their chest out with pride when the colored soldiers walked down the street, it was a different story once they left the block. When President Woodrow Wilson declared war on Germany in 1917, hundreds of thousands of Negroes signed up to fight. But nearly all were stuck in segregated camps with bad food, no recreational facilities, and assigned to do hard manual labor. Only after the NAACP and other Negro groups fought a tenacious battle were a handful of them allowed to become officers. None were allowed to give orders to white soldiers.

I never heard any of the soldiers complain about their rotten treatment. They felt that if they did their duty and served their country loyally that maybe this would make things better after the war. They got part of it right. They did everything, and much more, to prove their valor in combat. Colored soldiers fought in some of the toughest battles in France. Many were killed and wounded. When the war ended in 1918, the French recognized their valor and did something that the Americans were reluctant to do.

They showered them with medals such as the *Croix de Guerre* and many other commendations.

I recall that when one of the soldiers who lived on our block came home nearly everyone on the block went to his place to celebrate. He had a huge medal pinned to his army uniform. It was so shiny you could see your reflection in it. On the table in the living room was a bayonet and knife that he said he took from a dead German. Everyone sat in rapt attention as he told his battle tales. There were mountains of chicken, barbecue, soda, beer and for some, even more lively spirits. The celebration went on well into the night.

The part we didn't get right about the effect of the colored soldier's performance was that there was no let up in discrimination. In fact, things got worse. Black men were beaten and lynched sometimes while wearing their uniforms. Even though Negroes had done their duty toward their country, many whites were even more determined to keep or put them back in their place. The Negro papers were filled with pictures of, and stories about, colored persons being shot and beaten, and their houses burned in Chicago and Washington, D.C.

The one thing that was different this time was that the colored persons weren't afraid to talk about the violence anymore. They were happy and proud that some colored people were finally fighting back against their white attackers.

Democracy For Whom?

*A*t age 18, I took the examination for postal clerk. At that time there were no colored clerks in any post offices in St. Louis. There were, however, colored mail carriers. In 1922, I entered the postal service and was assigned to work the graveyard shift. I was elated to be working for the U.S. Government. But, I soon encountered blatant segregation. My first night in the cafeteria, I was tapped on the shoulder by the manager who pointed out a certain spot provided for colored workers. The whites sat on the other side and ate.

We colored workers could thank President Wilson for that. One of the first things that he did as president in 1912 was to sign an executive order that forbade blacks from eating with whites in the cafeterias and using restrooms designated for "whites only." Wilson wasn't finished with us. He was silent when Congress tried to pass more segregation bills than ever in American history during his first term in office.

I don't know whether my mother voted for Wilson or not. But I recall that there were big letters on the front of the *Argus* on election day that said: "WILSON ELECTED PRESIDENT." I don't know if the paper actually endorsed Wilson, since most blacks then voted for the Republicans. However, he was the first Democrat to get a significant number of black votes. He got their votes by making a few promises to give us fair treatment. We should have known better. He was a Southerner. And he, too, wasn't about to do anything to anger the South.

When you checked in for your shift at the post office you would go to the detail desk where the clerk would be a hard-nosed white guy who assigned the colored back-breaking details such as loading the stamp table or primary mail separation. You stood at this case the entire work shift. During those years, there was no such thing as a break until lunch. If I had to go to the restroom, I was required to sign out at the detail desk. The colored clerks had no representation like the whites who were represented by the American Federation of Labor (AFL). This was the only major association of labor unions in existence at the time.

Almost all the unions in the AFL were lily-white. They had formal clauses in their by-laws that flat out said no colored workers were allowed to join. The only union that I heard anything good about was the United Mine Workers. They had lots of black members. That didn't help any one of the colored workers in St. Louis because there were no coal mines in the city. Being kept out of the unions meant that we would be assigned the dirtiest jobs and received the lowest pay. The only time that changed was when there was a strike by the white workers. For a few days, the blacks would take their place. The minute the strike was over they would get rid of them.

Democracy For Whom?

The colored workers formed their own union called the Postal Alliance. We could not post any communications on the station bulletin board. It was more like a social club. Any grievances presented to the postmaster or general supervisor, more often than not, would be settled in favor of the white offender. There were many positions with more prestige that I applied for but I was always turned down. The same was true for the rest of the colored postal workers.

This was hard on a lot of the families in my neighborhood. My father, like almost everyone else in my neighborhood, was a laborer. He would come home with his face caked with sweat, his overhauls layered with grime, and collapse in the chair, or fall asleep on the couch. Most of these men made so little money that they lived on, or close to, the margin of poverty. They would constantly complain that they didn't know where they were going to get the money to pay the rent that month. Sadly, this constant struggle to make ends meet, eventually took a toll on my family. One day my father didn't come home from work. That was the last I would see or hear about him. And my mother rarely mentioned his name after that.

Fortunately, despite my father's desertion, we managed to scrape by. I don't ever remember my two brothers and two sisters going hungry, or wearing raggedy clothes.

If someone in the neighborhood was truly needy somebody would give them a basket of food or some hand-me-down clothes. We were poor but we got by because people cared for each other and pulled together to help each other.

3

GOIN' TO CHICAGO

Father we thank thee for the beauty of the world; all nature's grandeur, fresh air and sunshine, the seasons glad source change, for these O God we exalt thy name.

I listened closely to the stories that the men who left St. Louis to live in Chicago tell about the place. They would come back driving shiny new cars. They dressed in expensive looking suits, sported diamond rings, and flashed wads of cash. They would talk non-stop about the nightclubs, the restaurants, and the movie theaters in Chicago. They said that there wasn't any place that colored people couldn't go there. As I listened to their tales of a dreamland where everyone lived the good life and there was no prejudice, I knew that I wanted to go there.

St. Louis suddenly began to look smaller and more provincial than ever to me. It was still pretty much a deep Southern town. Colored people still couldn't work in stores or offices downtown, and could not eat in restaurants or go to clubs. They could not use any of the libraries, swimming pools, or recreation facilities. Many Negroes still lived in overcrowded, wretched flats, with no running water or inside toilets. The city's politicians were nearly all white and they didn't care if the streets in colored neighborhoods were cleaned, the trash picked up on time, or the street lights worked.

I put in for a transfer to a post office in Chicago. So that I would not loose my seniority, I had to find a clerk who wanted to move to St. Louis. It took a few months but I found someone.

At age 23, I arrived in Chicago in 1926 during one of the biggest snow storms that I had ever experienced. I was filled with excitement at being in the big city and looked forward to the future with great hope. But when I reported to the main post office located in downtown Chicago, I had my first unpleasant experience. While I sat in the Office of the Superintendent of Mail I watched white transferees interviewed in a traditional and very cordial manner, and then assigned their duties.

When it was my turn, the superintendent sharply

asked: "What did you want to come here for?" I replied: "As the transfer order from Washington, D.C. said, another clerk from this office wanted to attend school in St. Louis and it was my desire to work in Chicago. A mutual trade was granted." He grunted and told me I would be assigned to a night shift.

My first night hours were from 5:00 p.m. to 1:30 a.m. After checking in you got in line at the detail desk for assignment. If you were well-dressed with light colored clothing, the detail clerk would almost always assign you to supplying buzzer #1. I have no idea where this term came from. Buzzer #1 was a long sorting table for separating letters that came from dirty mail bags collected from street mail boxes. The mail was separated by size before being fed into the canceling machine for time, date, and city. Bulky letters (called fat stock) were held out. Mostly colored workers were assigned to work Buzzer #1.

---

*I*t didn't take long for me to discover that Chicago was no promised land either. Regardless of their income or status, Negroes could only live on the Southside north of 43rd to 29th streets between Ellis Avenue on the east and

Wentworth Avenue on the west and in another area called the Westside.

I was able to find a room in a boarding house crammed with new arrivals. They were mostly single men from Tennessee, Mississippi, and Alabama. Many of them had been sharecroppers, farmers, and day laborers. The apartment owners, nearly all of whom were white, had us at their mercy. They subdivided a three bedroom flat once, twice, three, even four times or more into sleeping rooms or what was commonly called kitchenettes— without the kitchen. They'd charge you highway robbery rates for the rooms. If you were lucky you could get meals with the room for extra, of course. In those places, you might find a dozen or more men sitting around the table shoving down food.

Seven years before I got to the city in 1926, there were riots in which dozens of blacks and whites were killed or injured. Chicago still hadn't gotten over the effect of the violence. The hatred between the colored and whites seemed to hang in the air. They avoided each other like the plague. One ugly result of this was that the cops were even more brutal and vicious in Chicago than they were in St. Louis. There were a few black cops that patrolled the neighborhood. They couldn't arrest whites, were paid less than white officers, and were kept at the bottom ranks of the department. They were considered niggers, too, and they took out their frustrations on us every chance they got. Some of them would think nothing of beating or even killing another colored person for even the slightest offense.

Many of them also had a nice little scheme to get a share of the policy rackets, the "numbers," money. Since everybody in the colored neighborhoods played the numbers, the cops knew who the runners were and what days they would make their biggest collections. They'd be right there to get their take. The more money that the cops took from the numbers runners in pay-offs the less money would be available for a numbers winner. This caused some resentment among many of the colored. The numbers was their field of dreams. Nearly everyone talked about hitting it big playing the numbers. Then they could buy a new car, quit their job, and live the good life.

If some black cops were brutal and greedy, they were only taking their cue from city hall. During the 1920s and early 1930s, nearly everything in Chicago was for sale and everybody seemed to be on the take. If a cop stopped you for anything, you had to shove a dollar in his hand. It was a racket and everyone knew it, and went along with it. If you wanted booze, a woman, to set up an illegal card or dice game, or even to get a petty job, and you had the cash or knew someone at city hall, you had it made.

Since I didn't know anyone at city hall and most of the

blacks didn't know anyone there either, we remained on the outside looking in. We had no black aldermen or state representatives to take our complaints to. The mayor and in most cases the alderman that represented your district was white. They would ignore your letters and calls. For all practical purposes, the colored were politically invisible.

That changed slightly in 1928 when we elected Oscar DePriest to Congress. He was the first black to get elected to Congress since 1901. And we loved him. He was a fighter, but he was also a really genuinely nice person. On weekends he would visit the churches—there were several hundred of them in the colored neighborhoods—swap stories with patrons at the barber shops and pool halls, or just stroll down the street greeting people. He always had a smile and pleasant words of encouragement for you. He made you feel like he really cared about you. As the only black in Congress, he knew that he was carrying a huge burden. We expected him to fight for the rights of colored people not just in Chicago, but everywhere.

Everyone liked to tell stories about how DePriest riled up the white folks in Washington, D.C. To them he was an uppity nigger and they tried to make life hell for him. He had to eat in a separate section of the cafeteria. He couldn't use the recreational facilities. I still recall the time that President Herbert Hoover invited DePriest's wife along some other congressmen's wives to tea at the White House. Many Southerners went crazy. Some states even passed resolutions demanding that the President never invite any colored persons to the White House again. DePriest didn't back down and this made us even more proud of him.

DePriest wasn't the only colored man who wasn't afraid to speak his mind. Robert Abott, the publisher of the *Chicago Defender,* was also fearless. I, and everybody else I knew, read the *Defender* from cover to cover. This was the best way to find out what was going on in town, who was getting married, divorced, who got shot, and what entertainers would be in town to perform. It was sold daily on street corners and door-to-door. But even more important the *Defender* kept the colored informed about the latest race news. If there was a lynching, for instance, the *Defender* would provide a detailed account of it. Abbott constantly talked about discrimination and tried to push the colored to protest against it.

The *Defender* also pushed hard for colored not to buy merchandise at the stores in our neighborhood that wouldn't employ us. In the late 1920s nearly all the stores on 47th Street and State Street were white owned. It was rare to see a colored clerk behind the counter. Many of the colored responded to Abbott's call for the boycott. It didn't take long for the owners to get the message and start hiring colored clerks.

The biggest race issue, however, for the paper then was the case of the Scottsboro boys. They were eight young black men accused of raping two white women in Alabama. They were sentenced to death. The *Defender* urged everyone to write letters and send money for their defense. Many of the colored churches and social clubs sent money to defend them. At the post office, the colored carriers and clerks took up a collection for the boys. We sent the money to the NAACP.

*B*ut that was only one part of the picture of life in Chicago in the early 1930s. The stories I heard in St. Louis about the good times to be had in the city weren't wrong. The colored didn't need to go downtown for entertainment we had everything we needed right in our own neighborhoods.

4

GOOD TIMES/BAD TIMES

*Father in the quiet of this morning hour we come to thee for
wisdom to view the world with greater understanding. Help
us to see the good in everyone. Deafen our ears to gossip and
slander, silence our tongues to unkind words, fill our hearts
with such faith and love for thee that we may do more perfectly the work thou has committed to our hands this day.
Thou who art the resource for every human need, entrust
us with wisdom, to serve our fellow men with
humility, unselfishness and compassion.*

*I*still believe that the Southside of Chicago had the
greatest night life of any city in America in the 1930s.
The fun began on 31st street. There was the Royal
Garden Ballroom that Louis Armstrong made famous.
South on State Street was the Grand Theater. Buck and
Bubbles, Bill "Bojangles" Robinson, the Fletcher Henderson

Band, Cab Calloway, Pearl Bailey, and many other colored notables would play there.

Across the street from the Grand Theater was the Vendome Theater. Erskine Tate's orchestra held forth there with such members as Eddie South on violin and Shirley Clay on Trumpet. Lines of people would form on State Street and curve around 32nd Street waiting to get into the theater. Traveling south on State Street to 35th Street, there was the famous liquor tavern called Preers. It was known for its hamburgers and hot dogs. Close by was the Sunset Cabaret. There you could see an all-night show. East on 35th Street there was the Apex Cafe. Louis Armstrong played with Joe Oliver another great trumpet player. Some nights you'd see Ethel Waters, Lena Horne, Billie Holiday, and many of the other big names sitting in the audience to catch the shows. Sometimes they would give an impromptu performance.

On 35th and Calumet Avenue, there was the Entertainers Night Club. South of the Entertainers Club to Oakwood Boulevard was the Grand Terrace. Pianist Earl Hines played with his great band including my cousin Eddie Fant on Trombone.

Near the Grand Terrace was Madam Malone's famous Poro College. You could buy every type of hair dressing and product. South of the college on South Park to 43rd Street, west on 43rd between South Park and Jackson Park, there was the famous Chin Chow Cafe where many of the big name entertainers grabbed a late night snack.

When you got to 47th Street that's where the big-time action began. We had a saying that if you wanted to see a colored person you knew, just stand on 47th Street long enough and sooner or later they'd come strolling by. It didn't make any difference whether that person was a celebrity, someone you knew back home in the South, or a neighborhood friend. Many celebrities hung out on 47th Street when they were in town. I often saw Jack Johnson, the Duke, Cab, and others walking down the street.

There was the Metropolitan Theater where the bands played all night. Across from it was Morris's restaurant, and Jim Knight's famous tavern and club. They were also popular hang outs for musicians and celebrities. Then there was the Regal where all of the vaudeville shows played. Fess Williams, Chick Webb were the big names that played there. They also showed many of the all-Negro films. There were westerns, dramas, musicals, and comedies. I saw films such as: *Harlem is Heaven, Temptation, Dark Manhattan, Underworld,* and *Harlem on the Prairie* at the Regal. Negro filmmaker Oscar Micheaux's company made many of them. But he wasn't the only one. There were several other black production companies that made black films as well. Near the Regal was the Savoy Ballroom. The big bands of Fletcher Henderson, Duke Ellington and Count Basie, and others played there.

My brother, James, played clarinet and saxophone in the pit band and his wife was in the trumpet section with Erskine Tate's band. My musical talents were a bit more modest than his, but I thought I played a mean saxophone and on occasion I did a little touring at smaller clubs, all-colored clubs, outside of Chicago with some local musicians. It was a great experience for me and the musicians. We had so much fun up on the bandstage that we'd have paid the club owners to perform.

Further south on South Park to 51st Street was Providence Hospital where Dr. Daniel Williams performed the first heart transplant. This was also the hospital where my son, Earl, was born. South of there was Washington Park. The homeless lived in the park during the early days of the Depression. They sold apples and peanuts to survive. South of there was Joe's Chicken Shack on 63rd Street. It was a very popular spot. When you went east of there on 63rd Street to Cottage Grove Avenue you bumped up against our imaginary Mason Dixon line. Negroes could not live past there.

Good Times/Bad Times

*T*he nightclubs stayed packed even after the stock crash in 1929 which many colored didn't pay much attention to at the time since most didn't have any stocks and figured it wasn't there concern what happened to rich white folks. But this changed as the Depression got worse in the early 1930s and we saw more of our friends and neighbors standing in the bread lines. People needed entertainment more than ever to keep their spirits up. They needed to laugh and have a good time. But they were rough times. It was nothing to see men and even some women sleeping in Washington Park on card boards, dirty sheets, or just bundled up in their tattered coats.

Most people, however, were generous with what little they had. If they had some food or clothing they would think nothing of sharing it with someone in need. There were soup kitchens on every corner and there were always long lines of men and women waiting for hours in the rain, snow, or heat to get the couple of slices of bread, bowl of soup, cup of beans, or any of the other surplus food items that private agencies donated and the kitchens ladled out.

If you were colored you could forget about trying to find a job in the early 1930s. Blacks couldn't drive cabs, work as sales clerks at any of the department stores downtown, the public utility companies, drive buses, or work in the construction trade unions. The only city jobs they could get were as road and street laborers. The colored policemen and fireman

41

could only work in the black neighborhoods. Things were so bad that the whites who used to laugh at and turn their noses up at what they called "nigger jobs" such as garbage collectors, elevator operators, busboys, porters waiters, street cleaners, and ditch diggers, now demanded that the colored be fired from those jobs and they be given to them. Many employers did fire them and the whites would snatch those jobs up as fast as they could.

Losing these jobs made us even more invisible in the work force than before. About one out of every two working colored persons were out of a job. There were, however, four types of jobs that were considered elite jobs during the Depression. They were railroad porter, fireman, and policeman, and the job I had, working at the post office. A colored man with a post office job was considered a rich and a well-educated man. Many of the men that I worked with in the post office then had masters degrees, and even some had a Ph.D. We had loads of colored people in the post office working on degrees in medicine and the law. Because of discrimination they couldn't find work in the other professions.

So, people knew that a colored person in the post office was somebody special. Everyone wanted to be your friend. Some even claimed to be distant relatives. They always had a sad story about being close to being evicted from their apartment, or not having any food. Their hand was out to touch you up for a loan. If I could I'd try to fill their hand.

5

NEW DEAL A COMIN'

O Lord almighty and most merciful Father as we begin this day, by thanking you for it, may we use it well.

We pray that thou will be pleased with the words we speak, and the way we behave. We ask therefore for wisdom in making decisions, for strength in resisting evil, for patience in dealing with people, in the quiet of this morning hour, we come to thee for wisdom, and greater understanding.

I also noted during those Depression years that more colored people began taking a greater interest in politics. There were days when I would walk through Washington Park on the way home from the post office. I'd see guys standing on the top of little battered milk crates that they had turned into soap box platforms. Some would

Earl Hutchinson, Sr.

call the white man all kinds of names and say that we should go back to Africa. They were the followers of Marcus Garvey. They would wear all kinds of outfits made up to look like military uniforms.

Others would be screaming that the only way the colored would ever get a decent job and put an end to lynching was to get rid of capitalism. All of the soap box orators stood beside each other trying to outdo one another. While they would always get a small crowd around them when they got through speaking, most of those listening would quickly walk away and that would pretty much be the end of it.

I recall one little brown-skinned man who tried really hard to get a following. His name was Elijah Poole, but he insisted on being called Elijah Muhammad. He wore a funny round hat. He often came into the post office to get checks and money orders. This was common then since most blacks did not have bank accounts. They used the post office for all their financial transactions. He would say how the white man and Negro preachers were to blame for all the problems of colored people. All they do is take your money, talk about God, and live high and mighty.

Many of my customers would laugh and snicker at him as that crazy man. He claimed that the only true religion for blacks was Islam. He had a small storefront office that he

44

called his temple. It was a few blocks from the post office. He even invited me to come to his temple to hear the true word.

I was a devout Baptist then so his talk of Islam had no attraction for me nor for most other colored either. He didn't help his case with most Negroes when some of his followers clashed with police at a funeral in 1935 for one of their members and were thrown in jail. This was big news in the *Defender* at the time. I thought Elijah Muhammad was just another "jack-leg" preacher that had come up with a different hustle. They were all over the place then. Some preached salvation in beat up storefronts or their flats. Some held forth in the park, on street corners, in empty lots or just about anyplace they could get a few people to listen to them. I figured that this was the easiest, and for some the only way, they could make a quick buck. As it turned out to my surprise, Elijah Poole, better known as Elijah Muhammad, would one day become more than just another "jack-leg" preacher.

---

*T*here were several men that I and most colored people admired more than anybody else in those days. The first was singer-actor Paul Robeson. The first movie I saw him

in was *Emperor Jones* in 1933. It played at the Regal
Theatre. The place was always packed. The women especially were crazy about him. When he came to town he
would often put on a concert at a local church and it would
be packed to the rafters. Afterwards, he would occasionally
go over to Washington Park and give an impromptu talk to
the men and women living in the park. He would always
command a crowd.

The times I stood close to him I was struck by his size.
He was a huge man with a big booming voice. He would talk
about discrimination and the miserable way blacks were
treated. And he knew that we were with him because he
would say that I know that every colored person listening
to me is thinking the same thing I am about the way we're
treated. And, of course, he was right. Many whites and
some colored tried to smear him as a Communist. I don't
know whether he was or wasn't. I didn't care. I admired him
for standing up for us.

The second was Jesse Owens. The film clips were shown
at the Regal Theatre of him winning the gold medals in
1936 in Berlin and Adolf Hitler walking out in disgust.
Everybody cheered wildly. We felt like we were crossing the
tape with Jesse and that we were standing on the victory
stand with him when he got his gold medals. Later Jesse
moved to Chicago. I got to know him and his wife, Ruth,

very well. My wife, Nina, whom I met and married in 1937, was in the same social club with Ruth. Jesse and Ruth would visit our home often. It was a friendship I always treasured.

The next was Joe. Joe Louis that is. You always knew when Joe was fighting. The streets on the Southside were almost completely deserted. No people. No cars. In fact, the joke was that you could practically stand butt naked on the corner of 47th and State Streets and nobody would see you. People would fight and claw to get a spot near a radio to hear a broadcast of Joe's fights. The only other time the colored would huddle that close to a radio was when the *Amos n' Andy* show came on each week. We never missed an episode. But a Joe fight was something special. People would yell and shout every time the announcer said that Joe had thrown a punch.

When the fight was over, if Joe won, which he almost always did, people would run out of their houses screaming and shouting. Motorists would honk their horns, people would shake tambourines and ring cowbells. The local musicians would play their horns. The bars would be packed until all hours of the night. People would sing, dance, and drink, drink, drink. When Joe knocked out Jim Braddock to win the heavyweight championship in 1937 right there in Chicago, people were delirious. I don't think a colored person in town got to sleep that night.

Joe was not only our hero because he knocked out white guys. He was our hero because he showed that there was at least one place where we could be equal to, or even better than, the white man. His ring triumphs gave us a cathartic release for our pent-up fears and frustrations. For a moment you didn't have to worry about being unemployed, or not having a place to live, or being told you couldn't come into a place to get a cup of coffee. He made colored people feel that they were somebody and that was important during the hard times of the 1930s.

*T*he next man that many considered as our hero was Franklin Delano Roosevelt and especially his wife, Eleanor. We felt that they really cared about the colored people. There wasn't a day that went by I didn't pick up the *Defender* and see a picture of Eleanor or FDR, but especially Eleanor, laughing with and smiling to a group of black children, or shaking hands with some prominent colored person. She invited a lot of Negroes to the White House. We would cut those pictures out and paste them on the walls. We would even cut out the headlines from the papers when the Southerners called her "a nigger lover."

When the Daughters of the American Revolution refused to let Marion Anderson sing at their concert hall in 1939,

New Deal A Comin'

Eleanor had a special event at the Washington Monument for her. The day that the news of the event hit, many Negroes paraded through the streets carrying pictures of Eleanor. Everybody cheered them for carrying her picture. She was so courageous in standing up for us. This made us even more proud of her. When FDR met with NAACP leader Walter White, Negro educator Mary Mcleod Bethune, and other Negro leaders, we felt that we were finally getting somewhere.

I, and just about every colored person I knew, couldn't wait to get to the polls on election day in 1936 to vote for Roosevelt. The lines stretched around several blocks at some polls. There were so many colored trying to vote for him that the police had to be called out to direct traffic and keep people moving. FDR was so popular that it cost DePriest his job. DePriest was loyal to the Republican party. He made it clear that he wasn't going to change. I was deeply saddened when a Negro Democrat, Arthur L. Mitchell, beat him in 1934. But even DePriest probably realized that the Republicans didn't have anything to offer Negroes, and FDR did.

Many of us actually saw real improvement in our lives. With FDR's relief and job programs, a few more of us found jobs. This kept many colored from going hungry and getting kicked out of their apartments. It became common to see men and women around State Street painting fences, sweeping sidewalks, cleaning the gutters, picking up papers and trash in the park. Most of them got those jobs through the Works Project Administration program (WPA). They had recruitment offices for colored all over the Southside. What was even better they actually offered some black men and women training as typists, and in other clerical skills. It was almost unheard of up until that time for the government to train Negroes to do something other than be a cook or a waiter.

I also noted that fewer and fewer persons claimed to be my "relative" and "best friend" in order to hit on me for money. People were actually smiling more on the streets. For the first time in years they had a little money in their pocket and felt more confident about the future.

That's not to say that the hard times had ended. There were many days when I'd see people sitting on the curb with their few scraps of furniture piled up in front of an apartment they'd been booted out of it because they couldn't pay the rent. The lines at the soup kitchens didn't disappear. And colored still couldn't get any jobs as clerks in stores downtown, join many of the unions, or get any respect from white politicians. Many of the apartment buildings on the Southside were still just as crowded and dilapidated. Yet most of us fervently believed that things were finally going to change for the better.

New Deal A Comin'

Part of that change for the better was my wife, Nina. From the start of our marriage, she was determined to escape the fate of many colored women who in those years had to labor long hours away from their home as domestics in white homes. She took courses at a Negro beauty school that offered the Madame C.J. Walker hair styling and care technique. These courses were popular among Negro women in the 1930s. Madame C.J. Walker was the legendary pioneer Negro hair care entrepreneur and the first Negro female millionaire. She opened her own small beauty shop stocked with the assortment of Walker's relaxers, pomades, and rinses, dyes, even lye, and other hair products.

On Saturday the women would sit in her little shop to get their hair done for Sunday. That was promenade day when the Negroes would parade up and down 47th Street after church. Everyone wore their finest clothes. The women especially, made sure their hair was impeccable. Most colored felt that even though most were poor, they didn't have to look it. When my wife got through with the women they looked like a million. And more importantly, for the next thirty-five years of our marriage, until her untimely death from cancer, she made me, her family, her legions of friends and acquaintances, feel like a million!

Earl Hutchinson, Sr.

- Age 18, high school graduation.
- As a young man in Chicago, circa 1935.
- At Camp McCoy in Wisconsin,
  Army band early 1940s.
- At Camp Grant in Rockford, IL., Army
  band late 1940s, I'm first on the right.

- My wife, Nina, and I at a Phi
  Delta Kappa social in 1955.
- My wife, Nina, and her mother,
  Althea, in front of 6357 Greenwood
  Avenue, Chicago in 1951. Our first
  homepurchased in a white
  neighborhood.
- My current wife, Kathy, and I at a
  social in 1996.
- Taken in 1999.

—6—
FIGHTING A TWO FRONT WAR

O Lord fill our hearts with such faith and love of thee that we may do more perfectly the work thou has committed to our hands this day. Entrust us to serve our fellow men with humility, unselfishness, and compassion. We thank thee for strength and for hands with which to work. For all this we humbly thank thee.

---

*I*had much to be joyful about in 1938. My wife, Nina, gave birth to our first child. Like many fathers in those days I was anticipating a boy to pal around with, but it was a fine, beautiful girl born at Michael Reese Hospital. I was dearly devoted to her, so we named her Earline. I must admit that my excitement over the birth of my daughter was almost drowned out by the talk of another war. For almost twenty years I had been a member of the Illinois Eighth Regiment.

The Eighth was a national guard unit that had a long history of turning out top grade colored fighting men. During World War I, it was one of the colored units that won many battle honors for combat in France. When World War II broke out, most of the guys that were in the unit were anxious to see action. We believed strongly that the fight against Hitler was our fight, too. So did every other colored person I knew.

The NAACP, the *Defender,* and other black newspapers, ran stories and pictures of blacks in uniform and at training camps. This made many of us even more anxious to put on that uniform and go off to battle. The uniform was an instant status symbol in the neighborhood. You were somebody important. Many women would practically kill to date a guy who wore a service uniform. This made many of us want to join up to fight even faster.

There was a problem. While we badly wanted to fight Hitler, some of the service branches didn't want us. Not one colored man was in the Marines or the Army Air Corps. The Navy would take us but only as cooks and mess men. They were little more than servants for the whites, especially the white officers.

*T*he army wasn't much better. At every training camp, the colored recruits couldn't use the clubs and recreation facilities. In many of the camps they had set up separate clubs for the colored G.I.s. If you went to town looking for a good time, you had to ride the back of the army's bus, that is if they let you ride at all. You'd hear men home on leave grumbling about how they were treated. A lot of them were really mad about it. The riots that broke out in Detroit in 1943 made things even worse. I closely followed the news every day about the violence. The *Defender* was filled with pictures of colored homes burning and cars being over-turned and men being dragged from them by whites and beaten. I wondered if we would have to fight a war over there and a war here at the same time.

The colored soldiers still felt that they had to do their duty. The Illinois Eighth wasn't immediately called up for active duty when the war broke out. However, in 1942 it was redesignated the 184th Field Artillery Regiment. The word among the men in the unit was that we would soon see action. Soon after, I reported to training Camp at Ft. Sheridan near Chicago. I received an officers commission and because of my musical skills I was assigned to the Regiment's headquarters and service company. There were a dozen or so other all-white units at the camp. Even though our unit and the whites were housed in separate quarters, we often drilled together on the parade ground.

Our captain and drill master made it clear that he wanted our unit to be as sharp if not sharper in the drills than the white soldiers. He would bark orders at us during drills. If we missed a step we'd get chewed out. If someone's shirt was tucked out, they'd get chewed out. He was determined to do everything he could to prove that we could be superior soldiers. I stayed on active duty with the unit until the end of World War II. In order to continue playing in the band, which I wasn't about to give up, it was necessary to resign my commission. I did and reenlisted with the rank of master sergeant.

W hile colored men did their part to aid the war effort by enlisting in the service units it was also important for the colored to show their support for the war on the home front. Every weekend some church group, sorority, or social club would have a victory ball. They would charge anywhere from ten to fifty cents to get in and the places would usually be packed. They would sell victory bonds at the other door and before the evening was over they'd sell out. At the post office, every chance I got I bought a bond. I figured since I wasn't going to the battlefront this was the next best thing I could do to help beat Hitler and Japan's Prime Minister, Tojo.

But drilling in segregated units, buying war bonds, and attending victory balls wasn't good enough for the *Defender* and NAACP. They demanded that Negro troops be allowed to fight and be treated as equals. They persuaded Mrs. Roosevelt to back their demands. She went to bat for Negro soldiers and did everything she could to get colored recruits into all the services, especially into the air corps. We had some guys who were top flight flyers, who had trained for months at Tuskeegee and several other training bases in the South. They were desperate to get a shot at flying in combat. She stayed on the War Department about it.

While Mrs. Roosevelt, Walter White, and black newspaper editors pushed hard for the integration of the services, I believe that what really turned the tide in our favor was the threat by A. Philip Randolph in 1941 to shut down Washington if the government didn't treat us fairly in the armed forces and give us decent jobs in the defense plants. We constantly talked about the march. It seemed incredible to many of us that colored people could or would actually try to shut Washington down. Several of the men in the post office said that if they held the march they would join it. I felt the same way. The threat of the march paid off.

President Roosevelt signed an order barring discrimination in the plants. And Randolph called the march off.

After that the conditions started to improve not just for the colored troops but also for the civilians. More black women and men were able to get jobs in the shipyards and the aircraft plants. You heard some colored men even bragging about how they had built this ship or that plane. Several of my neighbors that worked in those plants bought new furniture and started eating out at restaurants. The colored aircraft plant worker replaced me and other guys that worked in the post office as the new financial kingpins in the neighborhood.

*T*he celebrations in the colored neighborhoods on Chicago's Southside the day the war ended were far bigger and wilder than the celebrations after World War I. Car horns blared, people blew whistles and rang bells, and traffic was stalled in the streets. If a man had a service uniform on he was mobbed in the street. Women hugged him and plastered him with kisses. At nearly every house on my block there were noisy victory parties. They went on late into the night and there was plenty of food and drink. It was such a joyous occasion that even the police who always kept a watchful eye on the colored whooped it up with everyone else. Everyone was caught up in celebrating the war's end. The colored soldiers were proud they had done their job. They weren't going to take any more stuff from the white man.

At the end of the war we lived in a home on Langley Avenue and my place of employment was in the next block at the Jackson Park post office. If there was an emergency, my neighbor would rush over to the station to inform me about it. A few months after Japan surrendered in August 1945, there was an emergency. My second child was born.

I rushed to Providence Hospital. At that time fathers could not be present in the delivery room so I had to sit in the hall and wait until the event was over. If the birth did not happen when I thought it should, my anxiety would rise. I would ask questions, but no one would give me any information. Finally, I was told that I had an eight-pound boy and that my wife was doing well. I poked my chest out, did a little jig, passed out my cigars, and proceeded to get a ball and bat. Before my wife left the hospital, the question arose about a name for my son. Our daughter was named Earline. The nurse said so what! Name him Earl. And that's exactly what I did.

Earl Hutchinson, Sr.

7

UNWANTED NEGRO

*Our Father in heaven and on earth, fill our hearts, with joy
and our mouths with praise as we celebrate the festival of our
saviors birth.*

*Have absolute sway as we approach the mystery of your
word appearing in the flesh of one like us. Stir up in our lives
the precious gift of faith. Set our hearts aflame with passion
for your kingdom. In his name, we pray. Amen.*

I didn't spend a lot of time thinking about the changes
that would affect the colored after the war. I was
preoccupied with my growing family. With the addi-
tion of my step son, Robert, born to my wife by a previous
marriage who had come to live with us, I now had three
children to care for. There was one thing, however, that I

did pay close attention to, Jackie Robinson. Every colored person paid close attention to Jackie's battle to make it in the majors in 1947. His first game with the Brooklyn Dodgers was like a Joe Louis fight. Everybody gathered around the radio to listen. After that whenever the Dodgers played and the game was broadcast, Negroes would be huddled around the radio. When the Dodgers played the Chicago Cubs it seemed that every Negro in Chicago showed up at the ballpark. The lines to get into Wrigley Field were blocks long.

While it was great that colored men would be playing in the majors, I was sad for many of the players in the Negro Leagues who would probably never get the chance to follow Jackie. Worse, many colored people stopped going to the Negro League games. I was a big fan of our Negro League team, the Chicago American Giants. I often went to their games at Comiskey Park. The games were always entertaining. The fans would bring their whole families and spend the entire day. They would gorge themselves on hot dogs, pop corn, and soda. It was like a big picnic. More important the Negro Leagues provided opportunities for Negro players and businesses to make money.

Almost all the owners, managers, coaches, trainers, and scouts were colored. They would spend a lot of money at Negro stores, restaurants, and other businesses. Within a few years after Jackie broke in with the Dodgers, black players were playing for most of the other big league teams. This wiped out the Negro Leagues. We talk a lot today about the evils of segregation, but there were a few pluses. The Negro League was one of them. Many colored people and I include myself still don't know whether it was a good thing or a bad thing when the League finally folded in the mid-1950s.

I did know that with three children and my wife's mother now living with us we needed a bigger place to live. State and Monroe Streets was then the center of black Chicago. The Negroes still lived on the south and westside of the city regardless of their status. This created a solid black area. We lived in an area called West Woodlawn. It was divided by Cottage Grove Avenue. To the east was East Woodlawn. All the homes in that area that went over to Lake Michigan had restrictive covenants in their deeds of trust. They forbade whites to sell their property to colored. Sometimes the property owners would record what they called a "gentleman's agreement" not to sell to anyone other than a white person. The courts routinely upheld these recordings.

Earl Hutchinson, Sr.

In 1946, my wife and I talked about buying a house in East Woodlawn. We found a white real estate broker who had a three story apartment building for sale. It was situated on Greenwood Avenue close to Lake Michigan, and not too far from the University of Chicago. We knew that there would be a restrictive covenant on the building. And we also knew that there was not much you could do about that legally then. You could file a court appeal when you were denied a house because of your race, but it would take years and cost lots of money to fight it. In the end, you almost certainly would lose in court.

In 1948, the Supreme Court outlawed restrictive covenants in the *Shelley v. Kraemer* case. This meant almost nothing in practice. The ruling just said that landlords and sellers couldn't legally enforce race covenants but that didn't mean that that they couldn't have them. In just about every deed on homes in white neighborhoods in Chicago there were race restrictive covenants and they were enforced by "gentleman's agreement." There was no government agency you could turn to for help.

In fact, the government was a big part of the problem. It was understood that all the new homes built and sold with federal money in the 1940s would be sold to either whites or colored in separate neighborhoods. There was no way white politicians would allow a building project that would accept colored to go up in a white area. The only good thing that might be said about being forced to live in a segregated colored neighborhood was that you often found a college professor, a doctor, and a lawyer living on the same block with a maid, porter, or a steel worker. You had every type of role model living side by side together.

Many of those professionals and laborers, however, weren't content with that. They wanted to live where their money would take them. If by some miracle they were able to buy a home or rent an apartment in a white neighborhood and they were able to move in, then they had to worry about the neighbors. The white neighbors would make life hell for them. They formed all kinds of "neighborhood improvement associations." Their aim was to keep the colored out of their neighborhoods. There wasn't a day that passed when I didn't read about some new "improvement association" that had been formed after a Negro family had moved into a house in an all-white neighborhood. They would do anything to keep colored persons from getting in, and if they got in, they would do everything they could to drive them out.

*T*he fear of harassment and violence didn't stop my wife and I from trying to buy the building we wanted in the white area in 1946. We decided to take a look at the building but we never saw the inside, just the outside. We decided to make an offer to purchase, but to do that you had to find what was called a nominee—a white person whom the broker would sell the property to. Fortunately, we found one. Consequently, the broker dealt with him as if he was the real buyer. The seller signed all the legal papers in the names of the nominee. My wife and I had to furnish all funds for the entire transaction. This was quite a concern for us.

We consulted a very prominent Negro attorney in Chicago. His first move was to have the real estate broker and the nominee meet in his office to go over the sale items. After the meeting we decided to proceed with negotiations. The next move by my attorney was to check out the broker's office to be sure it was a legitimate business. It was not uncommon then for some white and even colored con men to claim to be real estate brokers. They would promise a prospective Negro home buyer to find and sell them a home in a white neighborhood. They would collect their deposit and then abscond with their money.

After our broker checked out as legitimate, our attorney took us to search for the title to make sure the results met his approval. We searched the city and county records including the probate court to make sure this property was free and clear of encumbrances.

Escrow papers were opened by the nominee as buyer. The broker brought copies of instructions to my attorney's office. Every document pertaining to this sale was brought to the attorney's office. When the deal was ready for funding the attorney released the funds to close the sale. The deal closed and was recorded in the name of the nominee. The papers were returned to the office of my attorney. We recorded the bill of sale in our names. We were in ownership of the building but not yet in possession of it. The sellers did not vacate until about two weeks later. The broker turned the keys over to us and told us that we could move in but that we would have a problem with the neighbors.

We discussed it with our attorney and decided to move, but not to let the police know we were moving in. The reason for this was that in several cases we knew of, colored buyers preparing to move into an all-white neighborhood notified the police. The police then turned right around and notified the neighbors that Negroes were moving in. The neighbors immediately went to court and obtained an injunction preventing them from moving in. The courts in those days were on the side of the white homeowners and enforced all restrictive covenants. We were aware that a temporary injunction to prevent us from moving in could be in effect forever. However, once we moved in the burden would be on the neighbors to get us out.

On moving day I stood on the corner of 63rd and Greenwood and waited until the last piece of furniture was moved into the house. I then showed up. I informed the tenants in the second and third floor apartments that I was the owner of this building. They were sent notices to that effect previously. One was a professor at the University of Chicago and the other was a widow of a fireman. Then I informed the captain at the Woodlawn police station that I had moved into the building. I told him I was a Negro, a United States citizen, and an employee of the United States Postal Service. I also told him it was my desire that I, and my family, be given the proper protection. His response was "Don't worry about it. Nothing will happen."

The next day, signs appeared in bold letters in the window of every house on the street, "WE ARE LOYAL TO OUR NEIGHBORS, UNWANTED OCCUPANT AT 6357 GREENWOOD MUST GO." The effort to force my family out of the property began right away. The neighborhood association attempted to serve me with a subpoena naming my entire family in the building. I would not accept it. Every Friday they held meetings at a nearby hotel on the street in back of my property. There was a young white man living in the next block who stopped by and introduced himself to me saying, "Mr. Hutchinson, I want to let you know I welcome you, and their actions are such a disgrace." The next day this young man came by and said, "I will be moving. They saw me talking to you and my landlord asked me to move."

I contacted the city human relations department. The chairman then was former Olympic medalist Ralph Metcalfe whom I knew casually. He advised me to keep the department informed of any unusual action and every meeting of the neighbors. He said that they had a sympathetic white person who would attend their meetings and keep me informed as to what action they planned to take against us. The police had been assigned to watch the building. All they did was drive by, flash their lights on the building, and move on. This left the building totally unprotected.

This condition continued night and day. In the meantime, my wife and I stayed awake many nights. We jumped every time we heard a strange noise. I don't think we got a decent nights sleep the entire first year we lived there. I had a gun that I kept near the bed. I would have used it if I had to.

I also wrote a letter to Mayor Martin Kennelly and the chief of police regarding the actions, or I should say inaction, of the police. It was forwarded to the captain of the Woodlawn police station. Afterwards the police were much more visible. But not in the way that I wanted. They would sit in their cars in front of the neighbors' properties and fraternize with them. This still left my property completely unguarded. The situation grew more tense.

8

STANDING FIRM

*Father in heaven and on earth as we bow our heads and
humble our hearts, fill our hearts with joy and our mouths
with praise as we celebrate your name.*

I was then a member of the U.S. National Guard. This
was a unit of the Illinois 33rd Division. Our drill night
was Friday night. One Friday night I had just gotten
home and settled down when a four-by-four log was thrown
through the front window. The fence around my property
was also completely pulled down.

The police were called and a lieutenant assigned to the
riot squad responded. When he entered the building, he
flashed his light on his police badge to let me know he was
an officer so that I would not shoot him. I was furious and

in a mood to open fire. After surveying the damage, he decided immediately to station police on the property. The police reported in each day. Their instructions were to sit in the vestibule of my building and keep watch. They did for over a year.

There were many unpleasant incidents that occurred. The neighbors who lived to my immediate left had a child about the same age as my two-year-old son, Earl Jr. A wire fence separated our properties and the children would be in the yard talking and playing with each other. The parents would come out and send their child across the street to play or call her to come inside. I was determined to walk the street to make sure that there was no mistaking that a Negro family lived there. Walking from work one day, a middle-aged white man coming from the opposite direction said, "Son of a bitch." It was just the two of us on the street but I kept my cool.

On a very hot Sunday, a minister who lived across the street ran up and down the street hollering, "Those niggers over there got police sitting on the property and us white people don't have any police." I really had no compassion for the man who thought he would never see the day a Negro would live in the area. He was trying to incite a riot.

Every Saturday or Sunday I would walk with my son back to my old neighborhood. I wanted to expose my children to every organization which I was a member of.

This included the Masonic Lodge, Shriners, Elks, 154th Army Band, and the National Guard. My rank was master sergeant. I was assistant bandleader for the 178th regimental combat team. My son would be on the bandstand with me when I played a concert with the Masonic, Shriners, or Elks bands.

On drill nights, I would take him to the armory to watch our activities. On weekends I would take my son and daughter on drives through different parts of the city. I always made it a point to drive through white neighborhoods. I wanted to instill in my son and daughter a sense of what this world was all about. The meaning of the word family and life to me did not revolve around one small circle of individuals and one area of this world. All colors of people were members of the same race, the human race, created by God, our heavenly father.

In the meantime, the police still sat in our vestibule to prevent vandalism. I occasionally talked with them about the reason for this situation. The police would always quote statistics indicating that the highest crime areas were the Negro areas. My answer was always — not so. I told them that if they patrolled white areas with the same number of cops they did black areas and made arrests there like they do in the black areas the crime statistics would be high there, too. The results would show that the highest number of crimes were committed by Caucasians.

They also constantly asked me why I moved into this area. I told them I moved for the same reason that they would move. I wanted a bigger house in a better neighborhood.

In talking with them I realized that they believed everything negative that they had ever heard about Negroes. I also realized that their bigotry stemmed more from ignorance about us than hatred.

Meanwhile, the battle over restrictive covenants was still being fought in the Supreme Court. The neighbors continued to hold meetings to devise a plan to get the unwanted owner, namely me, at 6357 Greenwood Avenue out. The tenant in the second floor apartment said that he was moving out and advised me to keep my rear yard gate locked because they were going to burn my garage. I was also told by someone in the human relations department to expect more trouble.

Nearly a year after we moved into the building, I received a letter from my attorney informing me that the Supreme Court had outlawed "restrictive covenants." He said that he would go to court and seek to prevent the neighborhood association from filing another injunction against us. The police remained on guard at my building until three more homes were sold to Negroes. By 1950, nearly all the homes in the neighborhood were owned and occupied by Negro families.

Standing Firm

This continued the pattern that we are still stuck with in the year 2000. When blacks move into an area, many whites will run. I saw "white flight" everywhere in Chicago in the 1950s. Real estate agents, banks, and insurance companies loved it. They made a killing off of white fears of Negroes moving into their neighborhoods. They would buy the property as cheaply as possible from white homeowners and then quickly turn around and sell it to black buyers at the highest price possible. The same thing happened when I moved my family to another home in a Southside Chicago neighborhood in the late 1950s. The whites that were on the block turned tail and ran as soon as the blacks started moving in. The worst part of this was that this was all conveniently orchestrated by the politicians to preserve white neighborhoods.

*I*f neighborhood housing was segregated so were the schools. Many whites were determined that their kids would not sit next to a black kid in a classroom. The schools in the colored neighborhoods were in pathetic shape. Many of the kids didn't have current textbooks. The buildings were poorly maintained. And a lot of the teachers didn't care whether the students learned anything or not. When the Supreme Court outlawed segregation in the schools in 1954, many Negroes didn't get very excited about it. Even though the *Defender* ran stories about the case, no one shouted in the streets, or honked their horns the day the decision was announced. We all felt that it wouldn't do much for the schools that our kids went to, they would remain just as black, poor, and neglected.

What I, and many other colored parents who could afford it, did was to put my children in Catholic schools. They would take anyone regardless of color and they had a solid reputation for providing colored students with a good education. The first chance I had I put my son in a Catholic school and kept him there through his first year of high school in the early 1960s. The Catholics made it especially easy for colored parents to do this. They didn't require the parents to be Catholic. Most of the colored I knew that had their children in Catholic schools were Baptists or were members of the African Methodist Episcopal church. I had worshipped at Baptist and AME churches for more than thirty years. I was a deacon and board member at the Woodlawn AME Church. Many times I was called on to lead prayers at ceremonial events. So, I certainly was not about to change my religion.

There were, however, racial problems in the Catholic

schools. Many days my son, Earl, would come home almost in tears because of an incident that happened at school. The white kids would push, shove, taunt him and the handful of other colored students at the school in the halls, and threaten to beat them up. The priests there weren't much help. I would complain to the school principle about his treatment and those of other Negro students. They would tell me that they would look into it and get back to me. They never did. Still, he seemed to be doing well in his studies and as far as I was concerned that was the most important thing.

I thought about taking my complaint about my son's mistreatment in school to our alderman—by then we had several black aldermen—but I knew from dealing with some of the black politicians that they weren't anxious to rock the boat when it came to speaking out against discrimination. My congressman, Bill Dawson, was a good example of this. In 1942, he won his seat in Congress. I loyally supported him in every election in the 1940s and 1950s. Colored voters expected him to fight for our rights. And from time to time he did say the things that we wanted to hear. I remember he made a good speech calling for Roosevelt to establish an equal employment committee in 1944 (Fair Employment Practices Committee). He also spoke out against lynchings.

I recall that he called on President Harry Truman to integrate the armed forces. This was especially important to me having served so many years in the all-colored Illinois Eighth Regiment. I was still on reserve duty in the National Guard when Truman finally ended discrimination in the services in 1948. When he did we were overjoyed. Many of us wrote letters thanking him for his action. Truman got my vote for it.

Dawson, however, seemed to back slide on racial issues during the 1950s. I don't recall him publicly uttering a word when Emmett Till was murdered in Mississippi in 1955. This was a disgrace. The Till murder really tore all of us up. His mother lived a few blocks from us on the other side of State Street. She was a member of the Roberts Temple Church of God on State Street. I occasionally attended events at that church. When she brought his body back to Chicago for the funeral, thousands of people lined up for hours to file past the body and to pay their respects.

I wanted to see Till's body, but the lines were just too long. I saw women fall out in shock, cry, and scream. That week my pastor and nearly every other Negro minister demanded that we give money to the NAACP so that what happened to Till would never happen to another colored boy. I and some of the other Negro clerks at the post office took up a collection for Till. We turned the money over to the NAACP.

I also don't remember Dawson saying anything about the riots in Little Rock, Arkansas in 1957 that broke out when the Negro children were trying to integrate the white high school. Despite all the hatred and violence I had seen, heard about, and even experienced during my life, I was sickened watching on TV mobs beating up Negroes and turning over cars while the police stood by and did nothing. I remember the NAACP practically begged President Dwight Eisenhower to send in the troops. He finally did after the violence got way out of hand. His inaction didn't endear him to many colored people. I was happy that I voted for Adlai Stevenson against him in 1952 and again in 1956.

One of the reasons I believe that Dawson and some other black politicians in Chicago were not as outspoken about racial segregation as I wanted them to be was because they benefited from it in Chicago. It preserved Dawson's political position as the king of the Southside. He was a key cog in Mayor Richard Daley's machine. He kept a tight lid on everything in the colored neighborhoods on the Southside through his control of the ward precincts. He had captains, lieutenants, precinct, and block leaders. If you wanted a city job, to fix a ticket, get a street cleaned, or a political favor, you had to go through one of his people.

Dawson's people had their hand into everything including the annual campaign to elect the "mayor of Bronzville." This was a big event. Thousands of Negroes would cast their "ballots" for a candidate. The winner would be designated as the "mayor" of the Southside. He really took the job seriously. He would appear at churches, social events, picnics just as a regular politician would. Dawson and other Negro politicians made sure that the "mayor" was hooked into their system and would do pretty much what he was told.

I must admit that I was able to use the system to my advantage on occasion. For a short time my wife, Nina, was the ward precinct captain. If I needed something done all she had to do was pick up the phone and it was done. I was even able to get a relative who was involved in a drunk driving accident in which two men were killed released on bail with a phone call. Eventually the case was settled without him having to do any prison time. That was the way things worked if you were part of the machine in Chicago.

The big price for getting things done this way was that

you didn't dare protest too much about racial discrimination. If you did you'd suddenly find that your phone calls would no longer be answered and you'd be out in the cold. Fortunately, my job at the post office was beyond the reach of politicians. But that didn't mean that my battles there were over.

Earl Hutchinson, Sr.

9

ANOTHER PROMISED LAND

*Father we thank thee for the many blessings thou
hast bestowed on this universe. We thank thee for
health and strength and the vital spark within the joy of
being, the challenge of life itself. Father we thank thee for the
beauty of the world; all natures grandeur, fresh air and
sunshine, the seasons gladsome change. For these O God we
exalt thy name in your name.*

I know it's hard for many to believe this but as late as the 1950s Negro postal clerks were not assigned to postal substations located in white areas of the city. They were assigned to stations in colored neighborhoods or the main post office (terminal annex). Finally, after I made many requests for a transfer to a substation, mainly because of better promotional opportunities, my request was granted. On reporting for duty, I found the same conditions

Earl Hutchinson, Sr.

but on a smaller scale; Negro clerks did not serve the public in the capacity of window clerks. They could not sell money orders, stamps, postal savings bonds, or do anything that pertained to the collection of money. Their duties were mail distribution, parcel post, and publishers notices.

My tour of duty went from 10:00 in the evening until 6:30 in the morning. I distributed the incoming mail from the main office for the individual carrier districts for delivery to their districts. Eventually I was assigned to a day tour from 6:00 a.m. to 2:30 p.m. The interior of the postal station was a large workroom for the performance of the clerk and carriers' duties. There was a divided room called the cage that faced the street where all financial transactions were conducted with the public.

To work in the cage, an employee had to be bonded. The carrier window where the carriers would receive mail for delivery to patrons on their districts was located in the rear facing the workroom. The windows where the clerks conducted business with the public was in the front of the cage.

My assignment in the cage was the carrier window. My duties were to distribute mail, handle the mailbox keys, and return all items not delivered. After a period of time working the carrier window, I requested to be assigned to work at a window serving the general public when the next vacancy occurred. I presented my request to the white

84

station superintendent and, of course, I got the usual answer that it will be considered.

After a period of time a vacancy occurred. I reminded him of my request. I was informed that my request could not be honored because the replacement, a white clerk, had more seniority than I had. I continued my regular routine of working the carrier window and other duties. After a period of time another vacancy came up at the public windows. I again reminded the superintendent of my request to transfer. He said that he was keeping the window staffed on a temporary basis and would not fill the position with a clerk who had a regular assignment. It was obvious that there was an imaginary line drawn in the cage separating Negro clerks from public operations.

This was typical at every post office in Chicago then. There was not a single Negro clerk serving the public at windows that handled financial transactions. I was hardly the only Negro clerk that requested those assignments. They were all summarily turned down. The white supervisors probably hoped that we would get discouraged and quit or transfer somewhere else. I believed that you had to be persistent to get what you wanted.

During this period, another vacancy occurred at a window that served the public. I applied again. This time fortune was with me. I now had a supervisor who believed in fair treatment. He knew that I had worked hard and deserved the position. He approved my assignment request. This was a positive step forward not only for me but for other Negro clerks. I was determined to do the best job possible. I knew that I'd be watched closely by some of the white clerks and supervisors. They hoped that I would make a mistake. This way they would be able to say: "See, we told you the public was not ready for Negro clerks serving them in that capacity." I never gave them that opportunity.

---

*B*y the mid-1950s many blacks were coming back to Chicago and telling stories about a place where it didn't snow, never got really cold, and you could smell the scent of oranges in the air. They also said this was a place where there was little prejudice toward colored persons. The place was California. This stirred dreams in me of a land where you didn't have to always deal with racism. My wife especially believed all the tales she heard about California. All she talked about night and day was moving there.

I told her that I would consider moving there when I retired from the postal service. In the summer of 1955, we decided to visit very close friends who lived in Berkeley, California. We joined the Chicago automobile club. It had recently opened up membership to Negroes. We assembled all the information we could about California. We obtained the most important book needed for Negroes who traveled anywhere in the United States. It was called the "Green Book." The book contained a directory listing the places where a Negro could obtain lodging and food in each state.

The "Green Book" was the bible of every Negro highway traveler in the 1950s and early 1960s. You literally didn't dare leave home without it. You didn't need the "Green Book" to travel through the South. You knew that you couldn't eat in a roadside cafe or stay overnight at a roadside motel. The book was primarily for travel in the North and the West.

At the time the Howard Johnson lodge and restaurant chain was the only national chain that I knew that welcomed Negro travelers. But they were not as widespread in the 1950s. In many places there was no Howard Johnson and none of the other motels would accommodate you. I would try them anyway. If it was in the afternoon and I spotted a vacancy sign at a motel not listed in the "Green Book," and there were few cars in the motel lot, I would try to get a room. In most cases the clerk had an arsenal of excuses ready: "Sorry, forgot to change the sign," "The last room was just rented," "We're expecting a large group to check in later."

Many times Negro travelers simply preferred to sleep in their cars. I recall that there was a motel located in Wichita, Kansas operated by Caucasians. The owner said that we could sleep there, but could not eat at the restaurant or the bus station. Even though, all bus stations then were bound by federal law and regulated by Interstate Regulations, before 1962 there was no statute that required them to serve colored persons. We ran into the same problem nearly every place we stopped until we reached Denver, Colorado.

When we finally arrived in Berkeley, California in August 1955, it was so cold I had to wear my top coat with its insert. I stood in line at a restaurant on the Fisherman's Wharf in San Francisco and nearly froze. I knew then that I would not settle in Northern California. When we visited Los Angeles I felt this was a place more suited to my taste. The weather was mild. The city was clean. And there were no overt signs of discrimination. I still wasn't convinced that California was the place for me. I felt that Chicago had the greatest opportunities for the Negro. But I kept an open mind. My goal in life has always been to find a place that was free of racial discrimination.

When we returned to Chicago, my wife continued to talk about moving to California. When I decided to retire in

Another Promised Land

1960 after 37 years in the post office, I planned to work for an insurance brokerage company on LaSalle Street, near the Loop, which is in downtown Chicago. The winter of 1959 arrived with temperatures regularly below zero and snow so deep that it piled up halfway to the top our doorway.

After fighting the snow and traffic to get to and from the job, I was ready to make the move. My wife was very elated. The children were less than enthused. It meant leaving their friends, school, and the life they knew. We sold our building in 1960. We arranged to have our furniture shipped, grabbed our "Green Book," and headed out of Chicago on U.S. Highway 66 for California. We bid good-bye forever to Chicago.

This was the third time in my life that I journeyed in search of a promised land free of the burden of discrimination. I made these journeys to make America live up to its promise of democracy for a colored man.

I did not come to California to retire. I wanted a totally new career. I also wanted to find out if California was indeed the promised land for Negroes. A former associate in the Chicago post office had moved to Los Angeles several years earlier. He had established himself in the real estate business. He persuaded me to get my real estate license.

I got my license and began work for a black real estate broker. This gave me a first hand look at the rampant racism in housing in Los Angeles. The black real estate brokers were refused membership in the Board of Realtors. This was the trade organization of the real estate industry. They gave the black realtors no official reason for denying them membership.

Realizing the need for a trade organization, a group of black brokers met in Spring 1960 and formed their own organization called the Consolidated Realty Board of Southern California, Inc. They called themselves realtists to deliberately distinguish themselves from the white real estate association and the brokers.

I served on various committees in the CRB. However, the low and moderate income committee was the most satisfying I served on. The committee was responsible for trying to eliminate the racial iniquities in appraising properties in predominantly minority neighborhoods. As chairman of this committee, I insisted that complaints be detailed in writing to present to HUD and the VA in an effort to get them to take action. This was important to try and identify patterns and practices of discrimination. I and other members were determined to do everything we could to open up housing opportunities for minorities in the city.

The single biggest problem that confronted us was the practice of "red lining." This is the practice in which banks and savings and loans use zip codes to deny loans to homebuyers in minority neighborhoods. Then all the major banks such as the Bank of America, Chase Manhattan, American Savings, Union Bank, and many others across the U.S. engaged in the practice. Some lenders openly stated that they would not lend in certain areas. These areas were almost always Negro or Hispanic. This practice also made it difficult, if not impossible, to obtain insurance coverage for property in those areas.

I'm proud to say that the black realtists groups, the California Association of Real Estate Brokers and the National Association of Real Estate Brokers, played a big part in breaking down the barriers of housing discrimination. The associations continued to lobby for passage of the federal and state laws to prohibit red lining and housing discrimination. Even with the passage of the civil rights bills of 1965, and 1968, housing discrimination has not ended but at least it's no longer legal. I felt that in my small way I was able to contribute to the battle for fair housing in America.

Earl Hutchinson, Sr.

—10—
JOURNEY'S END?

There's an open gate at the end of the road.
Through which each must go alone. Beyond the gate, your
loved one finds happiness and rest.

I have often been asked at what point in my life I felt that my journey as a colored man through 20th Century segregated America would end. There were two times when I felt that. The first was when my son and I sat in the first row near the fifty yard line in the Los Angeles Coliseum in 1962 and watched Dr. Martin Luther King, Jr. and a parade of the city's top black and white religious leaders and officials march onto the Coliseum field for a civil rights prayer rally.

Thousands of people were jammed into the stands. They cheered loudly when King marched onto the field. This was a moment that I had long dreamed of. I had followed King's work closely since the Montgomery Bus Boycott in 1955. I heard him speak and had seen him on TV many times over the years but had never actually seen him in person.

I don't remember the exact speech King gave that day. I do remember that he and others were there to urge passage of the civil rights bill John F. Kennedy had recently introduced in Congress. This bill would end legal segregation in America. It would also end my journey through segregated America. I believed that King was the one man who could finally bring that journey to an end.

The second time I felt that my journey would soon end was when the March on Washington was held in August 1963. I watched every moment of the march on TV. I was moved by the force and emotion of King's words. My wife, friends, and neighbors talked about his speech for days. In fact, whenever Negroes got together King's speech and the march were the biggest topics of conversation. We deeply believed that we were on the threshold of ending the terrible conditions that I and so many others of my generation had lived through and had fought so hard to change. When Kennedy was shot, nearly every colored person I knew was depressed. We felt that he really wanted to end discrimination and that he would do everything to get his civil rights bill through Congress.

Journey's End

The Southerners in Congress did everything they could to torpedo the bill. It took a big fight by President Lyndon Johnson to get the bill passed. When he signed it I rejoiced because that meant that legal segregation was finally dead in America. I said a silent prayer to the great God that my prayers and the prayers of millions of others had finally been answered. I also realized that in watching and being part of so many important events that affected our people during the first half century of my life, it would take more than a penstroke on a piece of paper to permanently cleanse racism from America. It would take a revolution in the hearts, minds, and spirit of individuals.

Since the passage of the civil rights bill in 1964, I have seen many things change for the better for Negroes. Many Negroes hold high positions in corporations, important political offices, and key educational positions. They can eat, sleep, live, work, and send their children to school almost anywhere they want. But these changes have come with a price. Many whites have found some sneaky ways to perpetuate their system of racial privilege. Many blacks are still just as poor, live in segregated neighborhoods, send their children to segregated schools, and are still discriminated against when trying to find jobs. They get locked up in prisons in greater numbers, and suffer higher rates of disease than anyone else in America

Many of us don't help things by peddling dope, joining

gangs, stealing from and killing each other. Some of us either through ignorance or despair are trying to undo everything that King and those who fought to end segregation in America accomplished. I hope they don't succeed.

As I stand on the frontier of the 21st Century I think back to the day nearly a century ago that I started my journey through 20th Century segregated America. I think about DuBois's prophecy that the problem of the 20th Century is the problem of the color line. And my great fear is that the problem of the 21st Century will also be the problem of the color line.

But my great hope is that just as colored persons fought hard to end my journey through 20th Century segregated America, others will continue to fight to make sure colored men and women will not have to repeat that same journey through 21st Century America. I pray that God fulfills that hope.